D0955598

devotions
for pastors

Stan Toler

wesleyan
publishing
house

Indianapolis, Indiana

Copyright © 2008 by Wesleyan Publishing House
Published by Wesleyan Publishing House
Indianapolis, Indiana 46250
Printed in the United States of America
ISBN: 978-0-89827-387-8

contents

Courage	7	Health	67
Perseverance	9	Uniqueness	69
Revival	11	Patience	71
Principles	13	Integrity	73
Instruction	15	Joy	75
Mission	17	Failure	77
Leadership	19	Values	79
Ambition	21	Rest	81
Persistence	23	Morality	83
Choices	25	Commitment	85
Kindness	27	Faith	87
Unction	29	Friendship	89
Vision	31	Legacy	91
Harvest	33	Love	93
Servanthood	35	Gentleness	95
Example	37	Healing	97
Effectiveness	39	Lamentations	99
Consistency	41	Depression	101
Responsibility	43	Clemency	103
Fears	45	Support	105
Forgiveness	47	Self-Esteem	107
Parenting	49	Speech	109
Guidance	51	Authority	111
Compromise	53	Regrets	113
Unity	55	Purpose	115
Counsel	57	Devotion	117
Compassion	59	Affection	119
Greed	61	Busyness	121
Change	63	Disappearance	123
Discipline	65	Passion	125

What does the Lord require of you and of me? That's a valid question for every ministry professional. It was asked by the Old Testament prophet, Micah—and it was answered in no uncertain terms: "He has showed you, O man, what is good. And what does the Lord require of you? To act justly and to love mercy and to walk humbly with your God" (Mic. 6:8).

Yet the demands and expectations placed upon a professional minister of the gospel are as varied as the individuals in the body of Christ and the communities we are called to serve. These requirements from outside sources often have less to do with measuring up to God's standard and more to do with measuring up to personal agendas and earthbound concerns. In attempting to live up to these combined expectations (often in our own strength and keeping only our own counsel) we cannot help but fall short.

What we need above all is a sweet and vibrant—and close—personal devotional life before God. As that daily relationship deepens and grows, we will come closer to measuring up to his expectations—that we become authentic and humble leaders who model how to please him more and more each day.

That's where this resource comes in. On this sixty-day journey into what God truly values in our personal and professional lives, we will be challenged by short daily readings, Scriptures, and real-life stories. The goal of all these is to lead us into greater authenticity in our communication with the God who called us and ordained us as his fellow laborers. And we will learn to break old habits and shatter flawed ideas about what the minister *should* do and be.

Each day we consider a topic devotionally and prayerfully—and commit to following through by putting our Faith into Action—we'll draw ever closer to the Lord we serve. Our families, our churches, and our communities will see the difference our growing commitment to Christ makes in the real world. And they'll be drawn to follow where the Spirit is leading us.

So ask the question each time you read a day's entry, "Lord, what do You require of me?" Then put your ear close to the Word and listen for his answer. It will free and surprise and challenge you.

"Courage," he said, and pointed toward the land, "this mounting wave will roll us shoreward soon." In the afternoon they came unto a land.

—Alfred Lord Tennyson

At 9:02 a.m., April 19, 1995, Oklahoma City got a wake-up call—and *courage* went to work. For seventy-two hours, people from all over the world gathered to rescue those trapped from the terrorist bombing of the city's Alfred P. Murrah Federal Building.

Story after story began to surface of rescuers burrowing into the dangerous darkness and precarious pockets of debris—hoping for a pulse and praying for a miracle. Such a miracle occurred late that first evening when the weak cries of Diana Bradley, 21, were heard.

For ten hours she had been pinned beneath the rubble. Choked by dust and numbed by shock, she waited for someone to hear her. Finally relief came, but at a high price. Her leg was caught under steel and concrete. Knowing she would die before rescuers could extract her, doctors came in to amputate. No anesthesia. No attending nurses. No high-speed instruments—only a doctor with a sharp scalpel.

Three months later to the day Diana, wearing a prosthesis, held a news conference in Oklahoma City. She praised the courage of those who saved her life.

Where do you need courage today? Draw upon the strength of the Holy Spirit within and remember: Courage is a gift from God that enables us to see beyond the moment into the eternal eyes of our heavenly Father.

faith into action

Name the most daunting situation you face in ministry, then surrender control of that situation to God.

Great works are performed,
not by strength, but by perseverance.

—Samuel Johnson

A basketball coach tells his players on the first day of practice, "Being in good shape is never measured by how tired you become. It's how fast you recover."

Have you ever noticed friends who are a bit more persistent than you? When the pink slip arrives, when the car won't start, when the phone call is bad news, they stand fast and firm as if to say, "If the going gets tough, then I'll get going."

It is gratifying to know the famous Russian author, Leo Tolstoy, wrote five drafts of his masterpiece, *War and Peace*, before it was published. And the American novelist, Ernest

Hemingway, rewrote a passage from *A Call to Arms* fifty-one times before he was content. Often, greatness is measured less by talent than by tenacity.

There's a pastor on the West Coast who has this saying on a plaque in his study: "Hangest Thou in There." It's not only his personal motto, it's what he tells people at the altar, in the hospital, and on their worst days. It's not trite to him. It's scriptural and full of promise.

Is there a situation you're facing that is particularly frustrating? Perhaps this is an area where you can develop perseverance. Ask God for new strength to use the difficulties of life to develop an overcoming spirit.

faith into action

Call a ministry colleague, and encourage him or her to hang tough.

Hallelujah, Thine the Glory!
Revive us again!
—William P. Mackay

At the dawning of the twentieth century, General William Booth of the Salvation Army prophesied the church would experience the following points of departure if revival did not occur:

Christianity without Christ;
Forgiveness without repentance;
Salvation without regeneration;
Religion without the Holy Spirit;
Politics without God;
Heaven without hell.

> If my people, who are called by my name, will humble themselves and pray and seek my face and turn from their wicked ways, then will I hear from heaven and will forgive their sin and will heal their land.
>
> —2 Chronicles 7:14

Some years ago, a pastor reviewed Booth's words and cried out to God for revival. Finally, in desperation he asked a dear saint, "What will bring revival?" Without hesitation she responded, "Second Chronicles 7:14!"

The next Sunday the pastor spoke from 2 Chronicles 7:14, and shared the following formula for revival: Pray without ceasing. Practice holiness in our living. Love our brothers and sisters. Be diligent in outreach. Demonstrate generosity in our giving. Experience the power of the Holy Spirit.

As the pastor completed his message, people began to move forward, weeping and praying for revival. God truly came into their midst, and the church experienced revival unlike anything they had ever known.

Are you hungry for revival, or are you in a comfortable—or uncomfortable—rut? Why not follow this formula for revival? God wants all his people to be revived daily.

faith into action

Practice praying without ceasing for an entire day, asking God for revival to start with you. Talk authentically and regularly to God throughout the day about each revival factor in your life.

Methods change but principles never do!
—Elmer Towns

While planting a church in Florida, one pastor began to focus on what many call the principle-centered life. He turned to the life of David and discovered principles that led David from lowly shepherd boy to lofty king of Israel.

According to 1 Samuel 17, there were no giant-killers in Saul's army. A review of verses 15–51 reveals these Top Ten Life-Impacting Principles for Overcoming Giants.

10. Be faithful and responsible in the little assignments (v. 15).

9. Be disciplined and trim off excess baggage (v. 22).

> So David triumphed
> over the Philistine
> with a sling and
> a stone.
> —1 Samuel 17:50

8. Be consumed with the glory of God (v. 26).

7. Be committed despite criticism (v. 28).

6. Be happy in the place where I am serving (v. 32).

5. Be ready to point to God's history of faithfulness (vv. 34–37).

4. Be comfortable with my own gifts and personality (vv. 38–39).

3. Be confident in everyday battles (vv. 45–47).

2. Be aggressive and decisive when required (v. 48).

1. Be determined to have daily victory over the giants of my life (vv. 49–51).

David became a giant-killer because he practiced the principle-centered life. Make these principles part of your life today.

faith into action

Choose three of the ten principles, and write them in a journal or on a separate piece of paper. Turn each statement into a personal question by beginning each sentence with phrase "How does God want me to . . .?"

For peace of mind, resign as general manager of the universe.

—Larry Eisenberg

You can probably relate to the story President Ronald Reagan told about the reporter for the *Los Angeles Times*. He had received instructions from his senior editor to get photographs of a brush fire in the foothills of northern California. The instructions included hurrying to the Santa Monica Airport to board a small plane, taking photos of the fire, and hurrying back by noon with the story.

The reporter dressed quickly, rushed to the airport, saw the small plane waiting on the runway, drove his car to the end of the runway, parked, and climbed on board.

Off they flew into the clear blue skies. At about five thousand feet, the reporter took out his camera and said to the man flying the plane, "Bank right and I'll take some pictures of the fire." Then he heard the most frightening questions of his life, "Bank right? Why don't you bank right? You're the instructor, aren't you?"

Do you ever feel like you are the instructor, and you don't have a clue as to how to do the job? Take a moment to get God's wisdom for the difficult situations you are facing. And remember, he is in control of this universe and nothing takes him by surprise.

faith into action

Examine your heart, and identify what is the most difficult challenge you are facing today. Lift it to God in prayer, acknowledging he is in control of it. Throughout the day, as that challenge comes to mind, remind yourself in prayer, "It's in Your hands, God."

16

If one's mission is too small, too vague, too parochial, there is the supreme danger of ending up being driven by someone else's mission.

—Author Unknown

Organizations, marriages, families, churches, and governments are no stronger than their shared sense of mission. The mission of your church or ministry is not carried out until that mission is written in the minds of the people you lead.

When we use the word *mission*, we are talking about a foundational intention that gives meaning and direction to life. A mission well articulated will provide guidance to all who adhere to the organization.

Jesus Christ had a mission that he never once walked away from. Even when his closest friends and critics tried to dissuade him, his mission guided his decisions and values.

Jesus' mission? He came to seek and save the lost. Therefore, it is easy to understand why Jesus stopped by the roadside and responded to a blind man's plea, why he spoke to a despised tax collector who climbed a tree, and why he allowed a prostitute to anoint him with expensive perfume.

In a world where souls drift easily in the myriad of choices and distractions, we ministers would do well to develop a simple covenant between ourselves and the Father—a covenant describing what his mission for our lives is—and never walk away from it.

faith into action

What is your mission? Write it down, and make certain everyone who shares your mission has a copy.

The sign of a good follower is
that he pushes; the mark of a
great leader is that she pulls.

—John Maxwell

It is part of the American culture: at every commencement ceremony on every college and high school campus in the land, the featured speaker proclaims to mothers and fathers, "These fine students—your children—are our great leaders of tomorrow."

The trouble is, it's not true. Not for 99 percent of them, anyway. Face it—most people don't know the first thing about becoming, much less being, a great leader. Despite what you might read in the latest autobiographies, effective leaders are never born—they are made.

> If anyone would come after me, he must deny himself and take up his cross daily and follow me.
> —Luke 9:23

If you are asking yourself, "How can I better lead my people?" perhaps you first ought to ask, "How might I become a humble follower?" Here are six keys:

Failure. A good follower, hence a powerful leader, must risk failure—and grow from it.

Originality. Look for every chance to do things in a new way.

Listen. Nobody has ever learned anything by talking.

Lean. Become dependent on the guidance of the Holy Spirit, and seek the counsel of friends and family.

Obedience. It is never a sign of weakness to say yes to God.

Willingness. The hardest thing about following is making yourself do whatever needs to be done.

faith into action

Prayerfully identify one attribute in the FOLLOW list that is your greatest challenge. Determine one practical step you can take today that is counter to your natural inclination. Ask for God's strength and direction, and then do it.

You make up your mind before you start
that sacrifice is a part of the package.
—Richard M. DeVos

I have always marveled at Paul's proclamation that he had "become all things to all men" (see 1 Cor. 9:22). Most of us would settle for being something to somebody. Yet, we strive so often to be revered by all, knowing we will fail most of the time.

That ambition has been referred to as the walk-on-the-water syndrome. So often, the people we lead expect the miraculous, and we do not want to disappoint them. I nearly destroyed my health trying to walk on water. As I look back, I have learned the following:

> And everyone who has left houses or brothers or sisters or father or mother or children or fields for my sake will receive a hundred times as much and will inherit eternal life.
> —Matthew 19:29

- Know your limits.
- Consider the counsel of others.
- Don't let people put you on a pedestal.
- Make sure you are transparent and confessional.
- Learn the phrase, "I don't know, but I care deeply."
- Encourage your spouse to keep you humble.
- Listen closely to the still small voice of God.
- Remember: Jesus loved all men, but obeyed only his Father—not the urgency of the moment, the push of the crowd, or the whims of his disciples.

You're not a super-being, but you serve a super God whose powerful Holy Spirit dwells within you. Let him be praised and glorified through you as you do your best to obey and please him each day.

faith into action

Write two or three personal limitations that are especially evident in you. Beside each, write the name of a confidante who can help share your burden or hold you accountable to be humble over the matter. Meet with that person to seek his or her support.

Persistence is the ability to face defeat
again and again without wavering—to
move forward in the face of great trial.

—Author Unknown

Brett Butler was one of my favorite major leaguers from
years past, especially since he became the center fielder for
the Los Angeles Dodgers. He was scrappy, consistent, and the
consummate team player. He was a bit undersized for his
position, but the greater the odds were against him, the better
he played. He's retired now.

In the middle of the 1996 season, Butler was diagnosed with
throat cancer. They said it would end his career, but Butler
predicted he would be back before the season ended. Bravely,
he endured radiation, chemotherapy, and physical therapy.

> I press on toward the goal to win the prize for which God has called me heavenward in Christ Jesus.
> —Philippians 3:14

As he predicted, Butler defied the odds and returned to the starting lineup—ready to lead the Dodgers into the playoffs. His first night back, he went one for three and scored the winning run. It was a great victory.

Butler demonstrates that, even when things are not going well and challenges take us out of our game, we can hold our heads high, give God the glory, and be an inspiration to those around us. We cannot let setbacks keep us out of the game.

faith into action

Determine what is holding you back and keeping you out of the game. Ask God for his strategy to overcome every obstacle and move beyond any failure. Be persistent and press on.

The greatest power a person
possesses is the power to choose.
—Author Unknown

A recent birthday caused me to reflect over much of my professional life. *Should I have done things differently? What would I change about my life?*

These are my conclusions. First, I would have studied more. Second, I would have been more faithful in my quiet time with the Lord. Third, I would have been a better listener. (So often in ministry we feel inclined to "talk our way through.") Fourth, I would have given more attention to the present and spent less time bemoaning the past or fretting over tomorrow—for I missed a lot of happy todays. And last,

> Delight yourself in the Lord and he will give you the desires of your heart.
> —Psalm 37:4

I would have spent more time with my family. When you pause to think about it, they matter more than anyone.

If I were to add one more, it would probably be to take myself less seriously. If you have not already noticed, none of us is indispensable or infallible.

As I reread these thoughts, it occurs to me that it's not too late to change. I trust these days are going well for you, but please slow down and ask yourself what you would do differently. Take time off periodically to reassess daily, monthly, and yearly goals. This will help you keep your priorities straight and keep you focused of what God has called you to do.

faith into action

Ask yourself what one thing you would change in your life for the past decade, if you could. Write it down, and pray for strength to make this change a priority in your life this week.

If you can't say anything nice about
someone, don't say anything at all.

—Every Mom

R on had long hair when it stood for rebel, listened to
heavy-metal music, drank alcohol, and experimented with
drugs. He had tried church but was turned off by the zeal of a
few and the judgmental eyes of others.

One summer he was hired to work in a lumber yard in
California. He was partnered with a skinny, fair-skinned Christian
teenager named Joe, who thought Ron was cool.

Ron and Joe laughed, ate, and talked for eight hours a day. Ron
drilled Joe about God and the gospel, but Joe never pretended to
know all the answers. One day, Joe asked Ron if he'd like to

Do not forget to entertain strangers, for by so doing some people have entertained angels without knowing it.
—Hebrews 13:2

come over to his house—a beautiful home—for dinner the next night.

A couple weeks later, Ron got brave enough to ask Joe over to his small house in a poor neighborhood, where he introduced Joe to some of his favorite music.

As the summer drew to a close and Joe prepared to return to college, they both knew their days together at the lumber yard were numbered. As they walked out to the car on Ron's last day, he looked up at Joe and tearfully said, "A lot of people have tried to tell me about Jesus, but Joe, you're the first person who has shown him to me."

Kindness is a habit you never want to break. Is it one of yours? If not, why not begin cultivating it today?

faith into action

Ask God to show you who needs your kindness and how you can demonstrate it to them. It may be someone close; it may be someone you barely know.

In too many places, the bland pulpit
has called for its own demise.
—Grant Swank

A favorite course in seminary is The History of Preaching. Preacher wannabes love studying great sermons like "Sinners in the Hands of an Angry God" by Jonathan Edwards.

A preacher said that as a young man he often heard the older ministers talk about *unction*. It mystified and at times confused him in his early attempts to preach the gospel.

What is unction? It is that quality in language that excites emotion—especially strong devotion, fervor, and tenderness. But it is accomplished by God's sanctifying grace upon the one who is speaking his Word.

The spirit of the Sovereign Lord is on me, because the Lord has anointed me to preach . . .
—Isaiah 61:1

A candidate for ordination was asked by the credentials committee, "Would you be disgusted if we didn't ordain you this year?"

"Oh no," replied the man, "God has already ordained me. He's just waiting for you all to get the paperwork done!"

Unction to preach the Word comes from above. How do you experience divine unction each time you minister? The following spiritual exercises will help you reach a "God-moment" the next time you preach or teach:

1. Seek the mind of God in sermon preparation.
2. Pray for the presence of God in your worship service.
3. Invite prayer partners to pray before you preach.
4. Look to the Word of God as your ultimate source.
5. Be sensitive and obedient to the leading of the Holy Spirit before, during, and after you deliver the message.

faith into action

As you prepare to preach or teach this week, begin by seeking God's direction and sanctification upon your work. As you continue in the preparation, continue in prayer to God, dialoguing with him and his Word.

Visionary leadership will
challenge the people of God.
—Talmadge Johnson

Rick Warren led his great church from infancy to twenty thousand in attendance—in twenty years. How? Rick Warren is a visionary leader. By his own admission, "God gave me a vision to build a purpose-driven church."

Most pastors are not like Rick Warren. In fact, many pastors struggle with vision. But every pastor who is making a difference in his community has a sense of destiny that is driven by the leadership of the Holy Spirit.

Vision is a key to making an impact for God in an unholy world. Perhaps these simple steps will assist you in your search for a vision from God:

> Where there is not vision, the people perish.
> —Proverbs 29:18 KJV

- Spend time daily in prayer, asking God for his vision for your church or ministry.
- Study the needs of your surrounding community or the people God has called you to reach.
- Seek wise counsel from visionary leaders.
- Examine your resources.
- Accept what God reveals to you, and share it with your followers.

Henrietta Mears once said, "There is no magic in small plans. When I consider my ministry, I think of the world. Anything less than that would not be worthy of Christ, nor of his will for my life."

Think **BIG**! God does!

faith into action

Focus your prayer today on asking God to give you a clear vision for your church or ministry.

While the world has been multiplying,
the church has been making additions.

—D. James Kennedy

S everal years ago, while pastoring in a small Ohio farming community, Rev. Blake Willingham became concerned about the need for a spiritual harvest. It was during a missions conference that he opened his heart to serve as a missionary.

After much prayer, he realized God wanted him to see the world in the light of Matthew 9 and become a sending pastor rather than a foreign missionary.

The next year he traveled to Kenya and observed the plight of the Masai warriors. He then traveled to Bolivia and met with missionaries on the edge of the Amazon jungle. He went on to India, with its poverty and spiritual darkness, and to the inner cities of the United States. When his missionary journey was completed, he was a different pastor. He had a new view of the world!

It was only after seeing the need for the gospel firsthand that he began to comprehend what Jesus meant when he said, "Go and make disciples of all nations."

When Rev. Willingham responded to the call of Christ in Matthew 9, he became a sending pastor. What is God saying to you about the need for a harvest of souls in your sphere of service?

faith into action

Identify what steps you can take today to begin carrying out God's mandate for winning the lost through your ministry, and take the first one.

Service is an act;
servanthood is a lifestyle.
—LeBron Fairbanks

servanthood

Mary and Don were two of the funniest people in the world. Their marriage was full of laughter and love for each other and for those around them. Then one day Don went out one snowy morning to shovel the sidewalk for his next-door neighbor. He suffered a fatal heart attack, and Mary was left alone in their home that had echoed for more than thirty years with such great joy.

A group of college students from Mary's church adopted her as their grandmother. For the next year they dropped by to visit, shopped for her groceries, took care of her yard,

35

The Son of Man
did not come
to be served,
but to serve.
—Matthew 20:28

maintained her car, and gently make sure she knew they were around. She told everyone they were her angels.

It is easy to love others on paper. It is another thing to show the love of God to someone who needs desperately to see it. It takes work. It takes money. It takes time.

When we become Christians, Jesus calls us to be like him, and Jesus got involved with people—not just by addressing the multitude from the mountain top, but face-to-face and one-on-one.

faith into action

Are you serving only from a pulpit? If so, you are stunting your growth and depriving yourself of tremendous joy. Pray for opportunities to serve people in special and unusual ways.

God of goodness, give me Yourself,
for You are sufficient for me.

—Julian of Norwich

Several years ago at the National Association of Religious
Broadcasters meeting, Dr. Richard Halverson, Chaplain
of the U. S. Senate, told this most insightful story:

His small son was playing in the backyard with his
friends when the conversation turned to a "my dad can whip
your dad" routine. Halverson overheard one boy say, "My
dad knows the mayor of our city!" Another said, "That's
nothing—my dad knows the governor of our state!" Then
Halverson heard his son say, "That's nothing—my dad knows
God!"

> Now this is eternal life: that they may know you, the only true God, and Jesus Christ, whom you have sent.
> —John 17:3

Dr. Halverson reported that he slipped away from his place of eavesdropping with hot tears streaming down his cheeks. When he reached his study, he fell on his knees and earnestly prayed, "Oh, God, I pray that my boy will always be able to say, 'My dad knows God.'"

How important it is for us to be a spiritual example for our children, the same example Jesus was for his disciples and for us. He did nothing without the Father. He spent hours in prayer, garnering strength, courage, and wisdom to do the Father's will. Clearly, he showed us how to know God.

faith into action

If you want to know God more intimately, follow Jesus' example. Establish your own mountain of prayer, a special time and place to be alone with him each day.

Holiness is as essential to the spiritual
life as food is to the physical life.
—R. S. Taylor

A preacher was speaking in the inner city when a church deacon interrupted the service to tell the congregation that vandals had smashed several car windows and someone needed to call the police.

The pastor responded, "No, we're not calling the police; we need to fall on our knees and ask God to forgive us for not being more effective in reaching the gangs in this community."

What an example of holiness at work!

The Word of God clearly links holiness with effectiveness. The reality is, we cannot bring our service to God in unclean vessels.

The One who makes us effective in the premarital counseling session, in the hospital intensive care unit, at the graveside of a stillborn child, in the pulpit, and in the serving of the sacraments, is the Holy Spirit.

With the Holy Spirit's power through our lives, we are "prepared to do any good work" (see 2 Tim. 2:21)! He is the One who makes us effective in service. And he is *holy*.

faith into action

Ask God to show you any area of your life that needs to be purified and set right with God. Don't let any sin, fault, or weakness hold you back from all God wants to accomplish through you.

Lord, help me to show my
children your ways.

—David Vaughn

As I wind my father's old watch, it is my prayer that I will live out the great lessons of life he shared with me. My friend, Jim Wilcox, reflects:

NOW

Then, I thought Dad was teaching me to ride
a bike without training wheels;
Now, I know he was showing me how to
stand on my own two feet.

Then, I thought he was teaching me
to construct a kite out of newspaper and
an old yardstick;
Now, I realize that he was encouraging
me to fly.
Then, I thought he was forcing me
to eat everything on my plate;
Now, I realize he was teaching me
the integrity of commitment.
Then, I thought he was coaching me
to throw and catch a baseball;
Now, I realize he was telling me that those
who play together stay together.
Then, I through he was helping me finish my
math homework for tomorrow;
Now, I realize he was teaching me that learning
lasts a lifetime.
Then, I thought he was working for a living;
Now, I realize he was working for me and
leaving giant footprints to follow.

faith into action

Write down (perhaps in a journal) at least two Then and Now comments that you've come to realize about your Heavenly Father.

The ability to accept responsibility
is the measure of a man.
—Roy L. Smith

I read a survey stating that four out of five of those who sit in the pew at church expect their pastor and his family to live at a higher level of moral integrity than other people. The survey continued that few of them thought any minister would be able to measure up.

While this may be hard for us to hear, it is the world we live in.

From time to time, political scandals erupt—locally and nationally. Scandals and wrongdoings on a local level can be somewhat tolerated. However, scandals linked to the White

Watch your life and doctrine closely. Persevere in them, because if you do, you will save both yourself and your hearers.

—1 Timothy 4:16

House, the highest office in the land, are more difficult to accept.

The world watches the church and its leaders in much the same way as we all watch the White House. Having higher expectations, we don't give our President room for error—and neither should we expect to receive much slack from those who follow us. In short, the world is watching us. It is not the world you are trying to impress or please, but your heavenly Father. As you please him, you are sure to have a life-changing impact on those around you.

faith into action

Make an honest assessment of the standard you adhere to in word and deed, and ask God to reveal any area where you may be coming up short.

When I have fears that I may cease to be / Before my
pen has glean'd my teeming brain . . . / And think
that I may never live to trace / Their shadows . . .
then on the shore / Of the wide world I stand alone.

—John Keats

Did you know that the number one fear in the world today
is speaking in public? (And to think you may do that two
or three times a week, you daredevil!)

We are born with only a handful of instinctive fears, and
most of them are healthy—the fear of falling, for example. As
we grow older, we discover fears that exploit our emotions:
the dentist's drill, the cold doorknob, the child who misses
curfew, and the loud bang upstairs.

It is when our fears begin to take control of our lives that
we need to take action. At that point, fears are called phobias

The Lord is my
light and my
salvation—
whom shall I fear?
—Psalm 27:1

and ought to be addressed through counseling—or maybe a few parachute jumps from a small plane.

Fear is usually founded in the unknown and grounded in ignorance of God and his Word. It is the opposite of faith, and the Bible says faith grows as we hear God's Word (Rom. 10:17). Therefore, the best way to handle it may be good counsel, exhaustive study, and fervent prayer. Ask God to reveal the cause of your fear and empower you to deal with it resourcefully.

Why not release your fears to the Lord right now? Remember, you are not alone. Your heavenly Father understands and cares, and he is committed to your spiritual tranquility. After all, he sent Jesus, the Prince of Peace, so you could enjoy the peace that passes all understanding (Phil. 4:7).

faith into action

Prayerfully examine your life and identify fears that have been consuming and long-term. Ask God to reveal the cause of your fear and empower you to deal with it resourcefully.

God forgives and forgets. Wise is the
man or woman who will do the same.
—Author Unknown

Every day we have the opportunity to remember. We can look
back over the preceding day and see that God's faithfulness
is tangible: the sunrise over the neighboring lake; the merging
lines of geese honking overhead; the bountiful feast on the
dinner table; the night of peaceful slumber.

Meditate on the word *remember*, and you'll discover it
doesn't fit God in all ways. In light of his mercy and grace,
the word *remember* seems out of place. Think about it for a
moment and you'll become aware of the fact that the Lord
doesn't remember some things.

God said, "I will remember their sins no more." Incredible! No wonder this word seems out of place. God doesn't just forgive, he forgets. And there's more: He wipes the slate clean. He destroys all the evidence. *He doesn't remember!*

> Their sins and lawless acts I will remember no more.
> —Hebrews 10:17

In the ministry we are surrounded by people who have been devastated by sin. They can neither forgive themselves nor others, nor can they forget past wrongs. That's why we've been called to serve. People need to know that God's memory is short, that he's long on grace.

Today you may meet someone who is having a difficult time forgiving himself for some past failure. Remind him of God's forgetful nature. And if you need to, remind yourself to forget.

faith into action

Examine your heart for any wrongs committed against you that you have not forgotten. Prayerfully consider whether you have forgiven those wrongs, and ask God to remove them from your thoughts.

There is just one way to bring up a child
in the way he should go and that is
to travel that way yourself.
—Abraham Lincoln

A pastor came home from a tough day at the office and said to his wife, "I've had a bad day. Please, if you have any bad news, keep it to yourself." To which she replied, "Okay. No bad news. Now for the good news. Remember our four children? Well, three of them didn't break an arm today."

Parenting is an overwhelming responsibility. The older our children become, the more overwhelmed we can become. We often feel like a short-legged beagle chasing a rabbit in a foot of snow.

As a parent, we're to *provide* for our children and *protect* our children, but our most important parenting responsibility is to *point* our children to Christ.

I want my children to remember:

Mom and Dad love each other.
Home is a happy place to be.
We love people.
I am the apple of God's eye (Zech. 2:8).

If you are married and have children, take a moment to evaluate your schedule. Can you have lunch with your spouse at a set time every week? Are there days when you can pick the kids up at school, help them with homework, and celebrate at the ice cream store?

faith into action

Pray and ask God to show you how you can improve your family life by being like Jesus to those you love the most. Then schedule a date this week to spend with your children.

A journey of a thousand miles
begins with the first step.
—Confucius

A traveling minister in a strange town asked a small boy for directions to the post office. After receiving instructions, he thanked the boy. "You seem to be a bright young man. How would you like to come hear me preach tonight? I'm gonna' tell people how to get to heaven!"

The boy responded, "You're going to tell people how to get to heaven, and you don't even know how to get to the post office?"

Our journey of faith takes us in many directions. Add to that journey of faith the call to ministry and immediately you're on the scenic route.

In Psalm 143 David models a prayer that we must pray frequently to keep in step with the Holy Spirit and follow his direction for our lives. David realized that to know God's direction, he must *listen*. "Point out the road I must travel; I'm all ears, all eyes before you" (Ps. 143:8 MSG).

David also realized the need to *learn*. "Teach me how to live to please you, because you're my God. Lead me by your blessed Holy Spirit into cleared and level pasture-land" (Ps. 143:10 MSG).

Learning God's direction for our lives is a process—an education that never ceases unless we stop listening and learning. Are you listening to him as you go about your day? Are you learning his ways in all you do?

faith into action

Consider a path down which your life or ministry is heading, and lift it up to God—ask him for clear leading.

The man who always has to
be right rarely is.
—Author Unknown

A pastor in the Midwest who was known as a great leader
often told his congregations that he would not go to battle
with them. "I am not a fighter," he told them, "I'm a lover." Is
it any surprise that his churches grew and flourished under
such a philosophy?

Rhetoricians teach that persuasion is less an art of coercion
than it is the art of compromise. Resolution of most arguments
is found in the middle of the two points of view rather than in
either point alone.

When I speak of compromise, I am not saying you should compromise God's Word. But one of the troubling trends in our society is that we look at *personal* compromise as spiritual and emotional weakness, rather than its true position of strength and power. Finding a peaceful resolution in the center of conflict is the true measure of effective leadership and personal integrity.

Pastors who can mediate, moderate, and compromise will grow churches. Pastors who refuse to budge will fail, because they have chosen to entertain only their point of view (which, wise as it may be, is nonetheless fallen).

What conflicts are you involved in? Have you taken the time to listen to all viewpoints and consider all positions? Remember, Jesus told us peacemakers are blessed (Matt. 5:9). Take every opportunity to stop a war and be a peacemaker.

faith into action

What is the most recent occasion in your life where you have drawn a line in the sand and refused to compromise? Is it a moral issue that is directly and explicitly prohibited in Scripture? If not, prayerfully consider how you might bless through compromise.

Tying two cats' tails together does
not necessarily constitute unity.
—Author Unknown

There once was a church that had little unity. Despite their inability to get along, however, they reached thousands of people for Christ.

Although they were effective in outreach, this church experienced overwhelming obstacles. The church treasurer ran off with the church's money. The leaders were constantly making people mad. The associate pastor was impulsive and quick to put his foot in his mouth.

Finally, a crisis came and the church divided. Several members were forced to attend churches in other cities because the persecution was so great.

> I have given them the glory you gave me—the glorious unity of being one, as we are.
> —John 17:22, 23 TLB

Where was this church? It was the church in Jerusalem! They would have done well to follow these tips to develop unity:

- Keep your tongue bridled.
- Keep your promises.
- Praise more often than criticize.
- Value people more than things.
- Smile frequently.
- Discuss without arguing.
- Refuse to gossip.
- Laugh with people, never at them.

With these standards for your ministry, how can you go wrong?

faith into action

Examine the list of standards for unity, and identify which is your greatest challenge. Lift this before God in prayer, asking for his strength to give you the means to become a unifying force in your ministry.

Happy is the minister who finds counsel
in the presence of the Lord.

—Author Unknown

Being a minister is not an easy assignment. Thankfully, Jesus is the Wonderful Counselor, not just for the people we lead, but for us and our families. Every word of Isaiah 9:6–7 penetrates deeply into our being, reminding us the God of the universe is reachable and intimately involved in our lives.

It is said that God's power was always evident wherever Robert Murray McCheyne spoke. He was one of the great Scottish preachers of the nineteenth century, and everywhere he stepped, Scotland shook.

A minister went to McCheyne's hometown hoping to see where he had preached. An elderly gentleman escorted him to McCheyne's study and asked him to sit in McCheyne's chair. The man hesitated for a moment, then sat down. On the table was an open Bible. The tour guide said, "Drop your head on that book and weep. That's what McCheyne did before he went out to preach."

We would do well to heed the admonition of the elderly gentleman. Seeking God's counsel from his Word will not only strengthen us daily, but will be the life we impart to others as we preach, teach, and counsel.

Be honest—do you spend enough time praying over God's Word and seeking deeper revelation on truth from the Holy Spirit? If so, continue and become even more fervent. If not, do something about it today.

faith into action

As you study God's Word today, dialogue prayerfully with God through his Word.

Compassionate ministry is done one way:
one-on-one, with all your might, soul, and mind.
—Steve Weber

compassion

It was one of those windy, blustery November days in Oklahoma when everyone looks for the warmest place to hide. The ice on the ground made driving hazardous, and the vengeful sleet seemed to slash viciously at the face of each brave soul who walked the streets.

The pastor of a local congregation had promised to take two college students to the City Rescue Mission that afternoon. So off the three of them went in the pastor's old Buick. Little did he know how the afternoon would change him.

> I tell you the truth, whatever you did for one of the least of these brothers of mine, you did for me.
> —Matthew 25:40

Kyle and Brad were two of the soft-hearts of the regional university and not yet acclimated to the brutally cold weather. They had bundled up well for the excursion, which included a brand new sweater for Brad.

After a couple of hours stuffing envelopes for a fundraising campaign, they were treated to a warm broth and white bread lunch, plus a tour of the facility. As they were getting ready to leave the shelter and head back into the cold, the pastor noticed Brad lagging behind. When Brad finally met them outside, he was wearing only a light T-shirt.

"What happened to you?" Kyle asked.

"I just couldn't leave with so much when they had so little," he answered.

How often are you moved with compassion to the point of self sacrifice? If your answer is, "Not often," try seeing every person you meet through God's eyes.

faith into action

Ask God to bring a needy soul across your path today; then go to where the homeless tend to be in your community, and see how God's Spirit leads you in compassion.

Don't worry—be happy.
—Bobby McFerrin

Russian legend has it that there once was a man who lived in dire poverty. One day he heard of a faraway place that would change his life forever—a place of land, food, and wealth.

He found the leader of these generous people. "Welcome," said the leader. "All that you see is yours." The poor man could not believe his ears or eyes, for what he saw was greater than he ever could have imagined.

"How might I acquire a piece of land for myself?" the man asked.

"Tomorrow," he said, "when the sun comes us, you will be given four sharp sticks. From a prescribed starting point you may walk or run and stake out the territory for your new home. The only condition is that you must return to that same starting point before the sun falls below the opposite horizon. If you do not, then you gain nothing."

The next day the poor man walked and ran and dreamed and planned all day, planting the first three stakes miles apart. When he noticed the sun setting, he began to hurry, racing the sun, but his greed prevented him from winning the race. Exhausted to death, he was buried the next morning.

When the leader asked his people, "How much land does a man need?" They replied wisely, "Six feet . . . and no more."

faith into action

Examine your own ministry and consider prayerfully: are there greedy pursuits that I encourage or chase after in the name of Christ? Seek God's guidance and forgiveness if relevant.

The more things change,
the more they stay the same.
—Author Unknown

A re you a person who loves change? Or does the idea of altering the way it's always been send cold chills up and down your spine?

Whatever your reaction, know this: *change is going to happen*. It is inevitable and unavoidable, so there's no sense fighting every change. The secret to effective, productive change is in the first eight verses of Ecclesiastes 3. Read them today.

There is a story of the new pastor who, on his first Sunday, preached before any singing took place. Then, instead of passing offering plates in the pews, he asked his congregation to parade across the front of the sanctuary and drop checks and change into a giant pot. But the most shocking change of all came after the service was over. Instead of greeting his people in the foyer, he exited out the back door and raced them all to the cafeteria. He was changing too much too fast, and it wasn't long until he himself was asked to change churches.

Adjusting to changes in life may be the most difficult thing we have to do. There is almost always a sense of denial and anger before there is acceptance—similar to the grieving process. However, your confidence is in knowing God has your life in the palm of his hands. He is in control; and whatever changes are in store for you, he will always be there to guide you and strengthen you.

faith into action

What are some changes that are occurring in your ministry or in your personal life? Lift these to God and examine before him how you are responding to them.

Two roads diverged in a wood, and I—
I took the one less traveled by, and
that has made all the difference.
—Robert Frost

I n sports there's a thing called "two-a-days." Athletes are forced
to rise early and practice all morning, running sprints, drills, and
exercises until they don't know if they will find enough oxygen
in the air to survive. Then, after a few hours of recuperation, they
come back for a practice made even more strenuous by the heat
of the day in the late afternoon. No one likes two-a-days! But it
is not the coach's intention to kill his players. Two-a-days hone
them, prepare them, and enable them to excel.

Each athlete knows this rigorous training will give him or
her the edge. Disciplined athletes will not only go through

this once, but will return day after day for more. They will be ready for each contest, and they will succeed.

Discipline creates disciples. In fact, the two words come from the same Latin root, *discipulus*. One cannot become a disciple without being disciplined.

Discipline is not a negative term, as so many think. We discipline our children because we love them. God disciplines us because he loves us. Proper discipline is the balance between correction and praise.

It is the wise leader, the effective coach, the loving parent, and the Christ-like minister, who imparts necessary discipline into the lives of others.

faith into action

Identify painful discipline that God has brought into your life in the past, or that he's applying right now. Take this experience before God in prayer, and thank him for this expression of love to you.

Healthy is he who has learned
how to smile.

—Author Unknown

Are you battling the three B's of middle-age: bifocals, bulges, and baldness?

The secret to health—whether it is physical well-being, spiritual vitality, emotional stability, or psychological security is a fourth B—*balance*.

One who focuses all his attention on physical health to the neglect of other facets of his life, as might be evidenced by models, weightlifters, and hypochondriacs, can become self-centered and have little tolerance for those who are sick, challenged, or obese.

> Do you not know that your body is a temple of the Holy Spirit, who is in you, whom you have received from God?
>
> —1 Corinthians 6:19

Those, on the other hand, who concentrate solely on their intelligence, spiritual welfare, or emotional survival, may end up one of the sick, challenged, or obese. The key is to do all things with moderation and balance.

Instead of looking at health as the constant battle of the bulge—the all-lettuce diet, followed by seven hundred fifty sit-ups, followed by an all-liquid diet, followed by the New York Marathon—view it as stewardship. Just as you would never neglect the care and upkeep of your church's sanctuary, treat your spirit-temple with equal reverence.

faith into action

Lift your health to God in prayer, asking for his strength and healing. Then determine a balanced, practical plan to invest regular weekly time in exercise, if you don't already. Consider simply going for twenty minute walks—beginning today!

> You are an original. God has
> shaped you for ministry.
> —H. Norman Wright

D r. Charles Crow says, tongue-in-cheek, "God loves you . . . but people have a wonderful plan for your life." Often in ministry we have plans or visions that others thrust upon us. Sometimes, we unwisely attempt to import the plans and visions of other successful ministers, usually without success.

God is a *personal* God. He has a vision for you just as he has a vision for the minister next door. He's unique and his vision for your ministry is unique.

In the physical realm we wouldn't think of borrowing a friend's eyeglasses to solve our vision problems. We might

> I was not disobedient to the vision from heaven.
> —Acts 26:19

gladly accept the name and phone number of his eye doctor, but we would need an individual screening to determine corrective measures for our vision. Yet we go to conferences and hear how someone built a church or ministry, and we expect to build ours the same way. It won't work!

Our loving heavenly Father is willing and able to show us our "vision from heaven." This is the plan and purpose for *our* lives that he has ordained—not our parents, not our teachers, or any other human being.

faith into action

Today in prayer seek the Holy Spirit's guidance for your calling and mission, or reaffirm it if you already know God's guidance for you. Ask God to help you always remember your uniqueness in Christ and to guard you against distractions and detours. Affirm that you are to accomplish God's will for your life, not someone else's.

Patience is accepting a difficult situation
without giving God a deadline to handle it.
—Author Unknown

Have you ever prayed this prayer during an anxious moment, "Lord, give me patience . . . and I want it now!" Have you ever taken a crash course on patience? Do interruptions, inconveniences, and irritations test your patience?

Ministry is full of interruptions, inconveniences, and irritations—they come with the territory. The late night phone call after a car accident. A robbery at the church. A disgruntled parent in the middle of your sermon preparation. Irritable board members, irritable staff members, and board members who are irritated with staff members.

Be still before the
Lord and wait
patiently for him.
—Psalm 37:7

Sometimes it makes you want to change the words of "When We All Get to Heaven" to "When All *But You* Get to Heaven!"

The key to overcoming these trials is patience—a fruit of the Spirit. It is impossible to lead people without this Spirit-given virtue. Without it, the pulpit can become an artery of anger, the board agenda a strategy for revenge, and the preacher intolerant and ultimately unnecessary.

James 1:2, 3 (KJV) says, "My brethren, count it all joy when ye fall into divers temptations; knowing *this*, that the trying of your faith worketh patience." Keep that in mind the next time trials come your way—patience is being developed in you.

faith into action

Identify what current scenario is most trying to your patience. Confess in prayer to God that this experience is for the development of your patience, and thank him for the opportunity to mature.

Integrity begins with how I live
when no one is watching.
—Author Unknown

Integrity is learned and demonstrated in many ways. One way is when this boat we call our life is put into dry dock and what is above and below the water mark is fully exposed.

In these disruptive moments of life we are most likely to display the integrity we possess. Integrity is almost tangible. Whenever we encounter it, we know we have found trust. It is fascinating to see people who live by what might be called super-honesty, men and women who live at the soul-level.

Alexander Whyte was one of those men. He was one of the great preaching heroes of nineteenth century Scotland. One

A good name
is better than
fine perfume.
—Ecclesiastes 7:1

day he was approached by a woman who showered him with words of praise. He knew the woman was sincere, but he also knew these kind words were not his to receive. In response to this lady's remarks, he said, "Madam, if you knew the man I really was, you would spit in my face."

Integrity begins with honesty at the fount of life—soul-level! Can you be considered by others to be living at that level of integrity?

faith into action

Have the courage today to ask God to search your heart and reveal the changes that need to be made. Then make those changes, and watch your life become new.

Joy is found in the presence of God.
—Author Unknown

A gifted public speaker was asked to recall his most difficult speaking assignment. "That is easy," he answered. "It was an address I gave to the National Conference of Undertakers. The topic they gave me was, 'How to Look Sad at a Ten Thousand Dollar Funeral.'" Now that's a tough assignment!

But here's an assignment that can top that one: "How to Teach the Early Church to be Miserable." The early believers had a joy that was unspeakable! It was unquenchable, unfathomable, and unsquelchable.

I have told you
this so that my
joy may be in you
and that your joy
may be complete.
—John 15:11

Paul wrote from prison, "Rejoice in the Lord always. I will say it again: Rejoice" (Phil. 4:4). His joy was not dependent on his surroundings. His joy was dependent upon the Holy Spirit of God who produces joy within.

Jesus is the joy of living;
He's the King of Life to me.
Unto Him my all I'm giving,
His forever more to be.
I will do what He commands me;
Anywhere He leads I'll go.
Jesus is the joy of living;
He's the dearest friend I know.
—Alfred H. Ackley

Early Christians were filled with joy because Jesus gave them *hope* and *life*. Should we be any different?

faith into action

Prayerfully examine the depths of your heart for the joy that is beyond understanding. Ask God to renew, strengthen, and deepen joy in your heart in a way that is beyond understanding and beyond circumstances.

What we call failure is not the falling
down, but the staying down.
—Mary Pickford

Ted Williams was arguably one of the greatest hitters in the
history of baseball. He hit .400 and is now enshrined in the
Baseball Hall of Fame. But Ted failed to get on base six out
of every ten times he went to bat.

We often forget successes and dwell on failures. We forget
failure is never final, and by doing so we allow failure to paralyze
our ministry.

There are many things about our past we would like to
erase. Most of us, if it were possible, would change something
in our histories. Would you like to take back a promise broken,

> There is not a righteous man on earth who does what is right and never sins.
> —Ecclesiastes 7:20

a word spoken in anger, an action taken in haste, or a decision made unwisely?

Remember this: Failure is universal. James 3:2 reminds us, "we all stumble in many ways." Perhaps you are failing now in some area of life. But the key to getting past failure is to learn from it. Ask the Holy Spirit to show you where you went wrong, the root cause of your fall. Then work with him to fix what needs to be fixed and go on.

It's important to reflect on the fact that Jesus Christ loves you and believes in you despite your failures. See the exciting work he has for you. He has chosen you to spread his Word. And whenever you stumble, he will pick you up, brush you off, and set you back on track—brighter and smarter than when you started.

faith into action

Write down in a column examples from the past five years of failures you experienced. In a parallel column, write what you have learned from those. Then write beneath those columns one pursuit you hesitate to pursue because of fear of failure. Lift past and future failures before God in prayer, seeking his strength and direction.

Determine what is worth more and
what is worth less than life and
you'll find your core values.

—Jim Williams

The *Titanic* was called the unsinkable ship, but it sank in the North Atlantic on the night of April 15, 1912. The ship rammed into an iceberg, which carved a three hundred-foot hole out of its hull. It disappeared into the dark waters within two and a half hours, and of the two thousand two hundred passengers on board, only seven hundred five survived.

A story is told of one man aboard the *Titanic* who, as the ship was sinking, offered another man a fistful of money in exchange for a seat in the life boat. The second man took the money and the first man took his seat. The man with the money never made it back alive.

> For where your treasure is, there your heart will be also.
> —Matthew 6:21

One man valued money more than life, the other man valued life more than money. One man looked at the immediate; the other looked at the long haul.

faith into action

Prayerfully examine your heart and lift up to God your answers to the following questions: What and who do you live for? What and who would you die for? What is your first thought when you awake and your last thought before you sleep? What are your dreams? What is your treasure in life? The answers to these questions will show you what your values are. Do you like them?

To overcome stress, enjoy a day off.
—Author Unknown

God modeled rest for us at creation. He created the world in six days, then he rested on the seventh. Why? Was he tired? No! He wanted to teach us the importance of being refreshed by resting.

Unfortunately, Sunday is not a day of rest for most of God's ministers. We are Sabbath breakers! (Today, we call them workaholics.)

It is interesting that in Psalm 23:2, the shepherd David writes, "He makes me lie down in green pastures." Have you ever had to make your children lie down? They get so wound up that you

Jesus suggested, "Let's get away from the crowds for a while and rest." For so many people were coming and going that they scarcely had time to eat.
—Mark 6:31 TLB

have to force them to rest. Yet we never make ourselves take a rest as an example to them.

Although you may take a regular day off during the week, you still feel required to tend the flock during that time. Sheep get sick on your day off. Lambs are born on your day off. Family, friends, or acquaintances may hit a crisis and call for your counsel and prayer.

If you are burning the candle at both ends, you're not as bright as you think you are! Quit playing Super-Minister and delegate.

faith into action

Identify a staff member or lay leader who either is, or should be assigned to handle things on your day off. Then ask God to give you the strength and discipline to honor that day. If we don't come apart as Jesus and his disciples did, eventually we will come apart!

Learn as if you were to live forever;
live as if you were to die tomorrow.
—Mahatma Gandhi

He was my mentor for preaching. As a young ministerial student I followed his ministry with great enthusiasm. He could sprinkle the stardust with his oratories. Without question, he will be remembered as one of the greatest camp meeting speakers of the twentieth century.

Recently, my hero sat across the breakfast table from me. Having been removed from the pulpit, he was a broken man—a life in shambles and a ministry ruined by years of illicit sexual behavior that had finally caught up with him. At his age there was little hope for restoration to ministry.

> And do not grieve the Holy Spirit of God, with whom you were sealed for the day of redemption.
>
> —Ephesians 4:30

As the tears flowed freely, my fallen preacher hero asked for my forgiveness. I reminded him that I loved and forgave him. I emphasized that God in heaven had also forgiven him. He acknowledged that he was forgiven through the shed blood of Jesus Christ.

As I watched him walk away, shoulders slumped, I thought of the mighty cleansing power of God's forgiveness and grace. I then thought of the people who might never hear one of his inspirational messages because of his sin. I still think he's the best ever to stand behind the sacred pulpit.

I know my hero is forgiven by God—just as you and I are. But the consequences of his sin are a grievous thing. We must never forget this any time we are tempted to disobey God's Word or the leading of the Holy Spirit.

faith into action

If you do not have a human spiritual confidant, begin to go through the process of identifying someone who is local and a spiritual peer with whom you could establish such a relationship. If you do have such a confidant, when you next meet, share the anecdote from this devotional and then discuss with this person what the ramifications of such sin would be in your world, to your ministry. Pray together for your protection.

You've got to stand for something,
or you'll fall for anything!

—Aaron Tippin

The words of this African pastor have traveled millions of miles, reflecting the commitment level of God-ordained ministry.

"I'm part of the fellowship of the unashamed. I have Holy Spirit power. The die has been cast. I have stepped over the line. The decision has been made. I'm a disciple of his. I won't look back, let up, slow down, back away, or be still.

"My past is redeemed, my present makes sense, my future is secure, I'm finished and done with low living, sight walking, small planning, smooth knees, colorless dreams, tamed visions, mundane talking, cheap living, and dwarfed goals.

"I no longer need preeminence, prosperity, position, promotions, plaudits, or popularity. I don't have to be right, first, tops, recognized, praised, regarded, or rewarded. I now live by faith, lean on His presence, walk by patience, lift by prayer, and labor by power.

"I won't give up, shut up, let up, until I have stayed up, stored up, prayed up, paid up, preached up for the cause of Christ. I am a disciple of Jesus. I must go 'til he comes, give 'til I drop, preach 'til all know, and work 'til he stops me. And when he comes for his own, he will have no problem recognizing me—my banner will be clear!"

faith into action

Read through this proclamation aloud to yourself. As you read, ask God to search your heart to identify any descriptions where your attitude or commitment doesn't measure up.

Change your thoughts,
and change your world!
—Norman Vincent Peale

While speaking at a mission's conference in Orlando, Florida, I was impressed with a seven-year-old boy seated on the front row listening intently. I had a flashback to the hills of West Virginia where I grew up, for it was at age seven that I received my call to preach the gospel while seated on the front row of a service.

I watched the boy as he responded to his pastor's invitation to fill out a faith promise and commit to give on a systematic basis to the cause of world evangelism. Little did I know that he had pledged twenty dollars.

As I prepared to leave the conference and go to the airport I felt strangely impressed to give his grandfather a humorous book I had written. I carefully signed the book, placed a twenty dollar bill inside, and gave it to his grandfather to give to him. I really wasn't sure why I did it—I just felt it!

At the evening service, the grandfather gave the book to the little boy, not knowing that I had placed the money inside the cover. Moments later, believing God had placed the money in my book for him, the boy joyfully proclaimed that God had performed a miracle, promptly paid his pledge, and shared his miracle of faith with the other believers.

And it was a miracle! Even if I had not placed the twenty dollars in the book, God would have provided it for him. How do I know? Because God honors the faith of a little child.

faith into action

Look over the past month or two and identify an occasion in which God provided. Recall the circumstances by which the provision was made, and consider whether rationales or explanations might have detracted in your own heart and mind from acknowledging it as a miracle.

The only way to have a
friend is to be one.
—Author Unknown

I have never enjoyed long vacations, because the longer I'm away, the more I think about church and home. Several years ago I learned to take crisp, brief vacations. I've found they relax me more than the monster trips.

One weekend my wife and I met old friends from college days in New York City and attended a Broadway play. We hated to say goodbye. As we were leaving for the airport, my college quartet buddy and roommate gave me a hug and said, "Old friends are the greatest friends!" I hastily wiped a tear from my eye and thought, *I'm too young to be this sentimental!*

I love people, and as a minister I've spent a great deal of time becoming friends with my parishioners. I have no regrets about being vulnerable enough to develop lasting friendships. It has paid huge dividends in terms of my ministry.

Today, there's lots of talk about networking. I would rather see church leaders focus on friendship-building. Whether you are a pastor or a traveling minister, a missionary or a volunteer church member, be a good friend to those God entrusts to you as family, associates, and bosom buddies. Remember, Jesus said the world would know us by the way we love one another (John 13:35).

faith into action

Write a short list of your close friends who, despite time and distance, you could still characterize as "sticking closer than a brother." Select one or two that you feel drawn to contact, and make a plan to do so within the next week.

The great use of life is to spend it
for something that outlasts it.
—William James

When Nashville First Church of the Nazarene celebrated one hundred years serving the heart of the city, I was among the four former pastors interviewed. Each of us was asked, "What would you like to be remembered for during your pastoral service as this great church?"

Carefully, I responded, "That I loved God, loved my family, and loved the people greatly." Until that moment, I hadn't thought much about the legacy I left that church.

How will we be remembered? I believe we will be remembered for the words we speak, the actions we take, the love we give, and the cards and letters we write.

Talk show host Larry King reported that during a hospital stay he received many letters and gifts. However, the one that touched him the most was a Bible and note sent by Pete Maravich, former NBA star. The note read, "Dear Larry, I'm so glad to hear that everything went well with your surgery. I want you to know that God was watching over you every minute, and even though I know you may question that, I also know that one day it will be revealed to you . . . because he lives."

The following week, Pete Maravich died. He will always be remembered by Larry King as a *caring* Christian.

faith into action

Ask yourself: How will I be remembered? If you are not satisfied with your answer, it's never too late to change it. Ask yourself how you want your family, friends, church, and associates to remember you—and then go make the memories!

If we do not show love to one another,
the world has a right to question
whether Christianity is true.

—Francis A. Schaeffer

Complete this sentence: My greatest aim in life is . . . How you respond determines the guiding principle of your life.

God's greatest aim for your life and ministry is love. Without love, all that you say is ineffective, all that you know is incomplete, all that you believe is insufficient, all that you give is inadequate, and all that you accomplish is insignificant.

LIFE - LOVE = NOTHING

Christianity is not a religion of beliefs—it is a lifestyle of love. The sign of a true Christian is not a crucifix, a fish, or a

Love the Lord your
God with all your
heart and with all
your soul and with
all your mind. This
is the first and
greatest command-
ment. And the
second is like it:
Love your neighbor
as yourself.
—Matthew 22:37–39

bumper sticker. The sign of a true Christian is his or her love for God and for His people. Galatians 5:6 says, "The only thing that counts is faith expressing itself through love."

An enemy of love is busyness. Clear the clutter out of your schedule, and let love be the order of the day. More than video games, trampolines, and the latest novelty toy, children need love. More than a new pair of shoes or a new dress, wives need love. More than a new set of golf clubs or a fishing pole, husbands need love.

For Christians, love is not an option, it is a commandment—sometimes difficult to obey. But God did not leave you helpless, "because the love of God is shed abroad in our hearts by the Holy Ghost" (Rom. 5:5 KJV). Draw upon God's love for you to love the unlovable.

faith into action

Who is the most difficult person in your life right now to love. Lift that person up before God and ask for his strength to help you be specifically and purposefully loving to that person this week.

You can walk hand-in-hand without
seeing eye-to-eye.
—Author Unknown

I f you want to be liked (and who doesn't?), it helps to be
likable. One of the most likable qualities a minister can
possess is gentleness. To be gentle means to be understanding,
not demanding.

Only two people in the Bible were referred to as gentle—
Jesus and Moses.

Proverbs 4:7 says, "Though it cost all you have, get
understanding." Understanding works everywhere—at home,
at the office, in a board meeting, even in traffic. God puts up
with a lot from us, probably because He understands us. If

Let your gentleness
be evident to all.
—Philippians 4:5

God can tolerate our inconsistencies and shortcomings, we must learn to understand one another. This is gentleness.

Gentleness is sometimes translated *meekness*. We mistakenly equate meekness with weakness. Like the domineering wife who said to her husband, "What are you, man or mouse? Go ahead, squeak up!" Yet the meek, the gentle whose strength is controlled by the Holy Spirit, is God's kind of person. Jesus said in the Beatitudes, "They will inherit the earth" (Matt. 5:5).

If you want to live a lonely, unfulfilling life, never admit you are wrong. Know it all. Always talk, never listen.

It is true, you will never see eye-to-eye with everybody all the time. But gentleness, which is a Fruit of the Spirit, can help you walk hand-in-hand.

faith into action

What circumstance might be occurring (or has occurred in your recent past) that would seem to require forcing your will on someone to accomplish the greater good. Determine how you could interact in the situation with meekness.

I heard about His healing, of His cleansing pow'r revealing. / How He made the lame to walk again and caused the blind to see. / And then I cried, 'Dear Jesus, come and heal my broken spirit.' / And somehow Jesus came and brought to me the victory.
—"Victory in Jesus" by Eugene M. Bartlett

As Jesus was on his way to help the daughter of Jairus, a large crowd followed him. In the crowd that day was a woman who had been ill for twelve years. She wasn't like the rest of the crowd. They were following Jesus to see what he was going to do for *someone else,* but she was following Jesus to see what he was going to do for *her.*

As ministers, we're sometimes like the crowd following Jesus. We are interested in what he can do for others, but rarely come to him for ourselves. It often takes a desperate situation before we "approach the throne of grace with confidence, so

He said to her, "Daughter, your faith has healed you. Go in peace and be freed from your suffering.
—Mark 5:34

that we may receive mercy and find grace to help us in our time of need" (Heb. 4:16).

Perhaps you have been ill or have suffered many years physically, financially, or emotionally. Why not exercise faith for yourself? Reach out and touch the hem of his garment just like the woman in Mark 5.

Do not limit what God can do for you because of your lack of faith, either. F. B. Meyer said, "Unbelief puts our circumstances between us and God. Faith puts God between us and our circumstances."

Do not allow your faith to become comfortable and complacent. Stretch your faith. Open your heart to Jesus, and give him the opportunity to say to you, "Your faith has healed you. Go in peace and be freed from your suffering."

faith into action

Lift to God in prayer any suffering you're experiencing, and ask him to free you from any enslavement it might be inflicting upon you. Affirm that his grace is sufficient for you to live in freedom.

When the whole world stinks, the problem
is probably right under your nose.
—Author Unknown

The town drunk was passed out on the sidewalk. Some kids thought they would play a trick on him by rubbing aged cheese under his nose. When he awoke, the aroma caused him to say, "This neighborhood stinks." He pulled himself up and caught a bus. Stepping on the bus he said, "This bus stinks!" Getting off the bus on the other side of town he said, "This neighborhood stinks too!"

When the whole world stinks, the problem is probably right under our nose. As ministers, we sometimes make some common mistakes: Instead of accentuating the positive, we exaggerate the negative. We allow facts to be replaced by feelings. We compare our ministry to another's ministry. And we blame ourselves for things that aren't our fault.

Common mistakes are blown out of proportion, one little thing on top of another, until finally we hear ourselves lamenting, "The Lord is like an enemy . . . he has multiplied mourning and lamentation."

At times like these, there is only one remedy: prayer.

faith into action

Pray the following: Father, forgive me for becoming more conscious of my problems that I am of You. Help me not to lose the focus of Your ministry. Replace stress with Your strength; replace my burdens with Your blessing; replace my pain with Your peace. Thank You so much. In Jesus' name. Amen.

Sally says to Charlie Brown, "We have to write a short
piece for school that expresses our personal philosophy.
So far I've written, Who cares? And Forget it."
Charlie Brown says, "How about, Why me?"
Sally says, "That's good, I'll fit it in."

—From *Peanuts* by Charles Schultz

Depression is not a new problem for God's ministers.
Moses, Elijah, and Jonah became so depressed that they
asked God to take their lives. David talked candidly about his
depression in Psalm 42.

Depression is usually a symptom of another problem.
Sometimes ministers get weary in well-doing. That is what
happened to Moses. God told Moses to delegate. "I will take
of the Spirit that is on you and put the Spirit of them. They
will help you carry the burden of the people so that you will
not have to carry it alone" (Num. 11:17).

> But O my soul, don't be discouraged. Don't be upset. Expect God to act! For I know that I shall again have plenty of reason to praise him for all that he will do. He is my help! He is my God!
> —Psalm 42:11 TLB

Fatigue, frustration, fear, and failure can quickly move God's ministers from the highs of Mount Carmel to the lows of a broom tree.

When depression overtakes you, consider these action steps:

1. Take a break.
2. Get some exercise.
3. Delegate.
4. Don't expect too much of yourself.
5. See your physician.
6. Talk to the Great Physician.

faith into action

Prayerfully consider each of the six suggestions, and lift up to God the one that for you is least likely to be (or the longest since) practiced. Commit to God when you will make it happen.

A sign at the entrance of a convent read:
"Absolutely no trespassing! Violators will
be prosecuted to the full extent of the law."
It was signed, "The Sisters of Mercy."

—Author Unknown

A four-year-old got confused praying the Lord's Prayer. He prayed, "And forgive us our trash baskets as we forgive those who put trash in our baskets."

That's pretty much what Jesus meant by his words in Matthew 6:14. Jesus went on to say in verse 15, "But if you do not forgive men their sins, your Father will not forgive your sins."

The church is simply a community of forgiven and forgiving sinners. Every individual who attends church on Sunday morning has fallen short of the glory of God. Some, however,

> For if you forgive men when they sin against you, your heavenly Father will also forgive you.
>
> —Matthew 6:14

have received God's free gift of salvation by grace.

Because God has forgiven you, you must forgive others. Why? Is this just another commandment "for your own good?" Yes! Bitterness, anger, or a critical attitude will bring sickness to your heart and eventually to your body. Forgiveness will make you free and release the Holy Spirit to bring healing to your life. So give up your grudges, grief, and guilt. Empty your trash basket today!

Ephesians 4:31–32 (GNT) says, "Get rid of all bitterness, passion, and anger. No more shouting or insults, no more hateful feelings of any sort. Instead, be kind and tender-hearted to one another, and forgive one another, as God has forgiven you through Christ."

faith into action

Examine your heart and memories—who in your life has been most in need of forgiveness? Look closely into your own trash basket and see if there are bits and pieces of the sin against you that still remain. Ask God to remove anything that remains.

As the yellow gold is tried in fire, so the faith
of friendship must be seen in adversity.
—Ovid

I have received many letters from ministers' spouses who are concerned about you, their mates. They write about your anxieties, the number of hours you put in each week, and how fatigued you seem. They write about your time at home— when your body is with them, but your mind is elsewhere.

They write about the financial pressures you carry, both for the ministry and the home, and how frustrated you get when there is just no more to go around. They write that they wish you had a close friend with whom you could be open and honest.

Lead me, O Lord,
in your righteous-
ness because of
my enemies—
make straight your
way before me.
—Psalm 5:8

So often they fear that you feel they don't really understand. They get frustrated when they see you taking heat from contentious believers who care more about themselves than the body of Christ. They worry about your kids and how they deal internally with what they see and hear.

But do you know what they write about the most?

They talk about how much they love you, how proud they are of you, and how often they pray for you.

You are blessed, my friend!

faith into action

Resolve right now a time and place that you will let your spouse know how much his or her support and prayers mean to you.

Most people are willing to take the Sermon on the Mount as a flag to sail under, but few will use it as a rudder by which to steer.

—Oliver Wendell Holmes

It happens every day. We turn on the television and see a well-dressed, silver-tongued orator who can preach circles around us. Incensed, and even a bit green with envy, we drive down the street and can't help but see that Dr. Smell Fungus has Mega in front of his church name.

Aristotle reminded the world that excellence is not an act, but rather a habit. If this is true, we must ask the question, "How do I measure up?"

Cathy Rigby was the hope of the United States at the 1972 Olympic games in Munich, Germany. She had one goal in mind—excellence! Before the games began, she prayed for strength to move her through the routine without making a mistake.

She performed well, but she did not win. She was crushed. She joined her parents in the stands, ready for a good cry. "I'm sorry," she said, "I did my best."

Today, Cathy recalls ten words from her mother that she will never forget. "Doing *your* best is more important than being *the* best.

The adage is still true—do your best and leave the rest to the Father. You have enough challenges in ministry without beating yourself up because another minister does something well. Your personal levels of excellence are found in your relationship with the Holy Spirit. He will let you know when you have done your best and when you held back.

faith into action

Determine the one thing in your ministry for which you have the highest expectation and standard of excellence. Examine your motives and the means by which you see it accomplished, and determine whether God's Holy Spirit truly is the driving force behind its pursuit. Lift it up to God, asking his strength to surpass your own means.

speech

We were able to see a perfect example of the old adage, "Loose lips sink ships," and its subsequent consequences when Fuzzy Zoeller, a veteran of the PGA golf tour, made an off-handed remark about one of his younger colleagues, Tiger Woods. He referred to Tiger as "that little boy" and urged him not to request fried chicken and collard greens for the champion's dinner at next year's Masters. His remarks cost him endorsements with K-Mart and participation in a tournament in the Carolinas.

We in the clergy can be some of the worst offenders when it comes to idle gossip about one another. I must plead guilty myself! We are intrigued by the misfortune of others in our ranks and spend an inordinate amount of time talking to one another about it.

The Zoeller and Woods incident reminds me of how careful we must be when we discuss the life and ministry of one of our own. Paul wrote in Ephesians 4:29, "Do not let any unwholesome talk come out of your mouths, but only what is helpful for building others up" I not only say amen to that, but I also pray, "Oh Lord, please help me keep my mouth shut!"

Zoeller issued an apology, and perhaps that might be fitting for many of us. Some of us need to apologize and some of us need to forgive those who have spoken ill of us. Every human being is tempted to talk of the faults and weaknesses of others— especially those they envy or dislike. But ministers ought to set the standard of godly speech.

faith into action

Recall the last time you know you said too much and regretted your own loose lips. If you haven't already, confess it to God and ask for his supernatural strength and presence of mind to guard your tongue.

It's hard, in a few minutes on Sunday morning, to offset the values presented through the media in the course of the week.

—William Keeler, National Conference of Catholic Bishops

As I think about the Easter season, I am reminded of a conversation Jesus had with his disciples. They were troubled over his words, "In a little while you will see me no more" (John 16:17). To help them better understand, he comforted them by saying, "You will grieve, but your grief will turn to joy . . . and no one will take away your joy" (vv. 20, 22).

Jesus' sacrifice would constitute both sorrow and joy for them. And in the name of the risen Christ—Jesus—they would find the power and authority to do the work of ministry after Jesus ascended into heaven.

When Jesus had called the Twelve together, he gave them power and authority to drive out all demons and to cure diseases.
—Luke 9:1

It is the same with you. Your authority, your power, and your credibility do not come because you are talented, gifted, charming, or articulate—but through the name of the Lord Jesus Christ.

The church can be full of itself, parading its organization and programs before the world. At times it is even boastful in its accomplishments. But be reminded of the words Jesus spoke in John 15:5, "Apart from me you can do nothing."

I wonder what it will take before we catch on to his admonition. He is risen! And that means that with him, we can accomplish everything he has called us to do and be all he has ordained us to be.

faith into action

Recall a recent success in your ministry. Honestly evaluate your own response—were you legitimately proud of the accomplishment? Did God's strength and means factor into your pride? Regardless of whether you thanked God for his work, do so again—thank him today for the success in your ministry.

From the errors of others, a wise
man corrects his own.
—Syrus

In the October 20, 1996, issue of *Parade* magazine, Dr. Billy Graham was asked by reporter Colin Greer, "How would you most like to be remembered?" Graham paused, then said, "That I was faithful to do what God wanted me to do. That I maintained integrity in every area of my life; and that I lived what I preached."

When asked if he had any regrets, Graham replied, "I would have spent more time with each of my children. Also, I would have studied more."

It occurs to me that this man, friend of Presidents and preacher to more than two hundred million people in live audience settings, is not much different in his wants and regrets than most of us.

For Dr. Graham the journey is nearing an end, but for many of us, there is time to make the changes we know we need to make.

Here are some questions to ask today:

1. How much time do I spend each day with my kids?
2. Am I careless in matters of morality and integrity?
3. Do I practice what I preach?
4. Do I have any regrets?

To finish well and have few regrets, we must daily evaluate every aspect of our lives.

faith into action

Prayerfully consider each of the four questions, and lift before God the one that weighs most heavily on your heart. Ask God for his strength, and commit to God when you will take the next step to correct it.

All great men and women became great because they invested time, talent, and ability in the care of others.

—Author Unknown

I thought the great snowstorm the country experienced one winter had finally caught up with me when my flight to Memphis, Tennessee, was delayed. However, I learned it was not due to the weather, but rather because one flight attendant was absent.

Evidently, the plane could not operate without three attendants, and there were only two. So we waited. When the missing employee was located, the boarding crew broke out into wild applause. Just think—the flight operation of the airline, hundreds of passengers, and a multi-million dollar aircraft were all grounded because of one person.

In many ways, your position as a minister can have the same kind of impact on the world you serve. At times, it may seem as though your presence is scarcely noticed. But consider what the lives of many individuals and families might be like if you were not there to offer counsel, direction, and every caution; to listen and pray; and to let them know they are loved and valued.

> From him the whole body, joined and held together by every supporting ligament, grows and builds itself up in love, as each part does its work.
> —Ephesians 4:16

The classic Christmas movie, *It's a Wonderful Life*, gives one of the finest illustrations of how each one of us has a tremendous purpose to fulfill, a purpose that is vital to those we love as well as those we may never meet. I call this the ministry of presence—just being at the right place at the right time.

Always remember: You really do matter!

faith into action

Identify three to five loved ones and imagine an "It's a Wonderful Life" scenario with them in mind. Don't simply consider what it would be like for them if you died. Imagine what it would be like for them if you'd never been born. For your own sake, as well as for theirs, praise God for your life.

Men will get no more out of life
that what they put into it.
—William Boetcker

M y mother often shared a story in children's church that illustrates what happens when we are devoted to a cause or mission:

A little boy had been taught by his father how to carve toys out of wood. As a result of his father's influence, the young boy became devoted to the idea of carving a complete boat. He built one complete with sails, rigging, and rudder.

The day came for the boy to test his wooden vessel for its sea worthiness. He carefully placed his boat into the large body of water. Suddenly, a gust of wind grabbed the boat and broke the twine that was attached to the vessel. Tearfully, he watched his prize possession sail out of sight.

Devoted to the mission of recovering his boat, the young boy visited stores that sold toy boats. One day he found his boat and purchased it back from the shop owner. His mission was finally fulfilled!

Ministry demands that kind of devotion.

Do you seek after the lost with the same fervency the little boy sought after his boat?

Are you completely committed to doing all you can for the kingdom of God, knowing that the end result is your mission fulfilled?

faith into action

Who is one person within this past year whom you have engaged but, to your knowledge, remains lost? Lift that person in prayer and ask God how you might cross his or her path again. Ask God to bring you together with that person, and if you can determine a way to contact, make plans to do so.

Acceptance is the truest kinship
with humanity.
—G. K. Chesterton

A Sunday school teacher once asked a group of adults, "Does anyone need a hug?"

Often when I counsel couples approaching their wedding day, I ask, "How were feelings of love expressed in your respective homes while growing up?" Many times they will respond, "We hugged. We said, 'I love you.'"

It is critical for those in ministry to experience warmth and affection with their families and fellow Christians. But unfortunately, it is the missing link in many parsonages. Many spouses confide that they just don't feel loved.

Be devoted to
one another in
brotherly love.
—Romans 12:10

Morris Weigelt often shares about a time he experienced deep depression. Once, I heard him talk about his hospitalization. He said, "It was very late at night and all of my insecurities and depression overwhelmed me. I got out of bed and walked the halls of the hospital looking for someone who was awake and willing to hug me."

With a great deal of pathos and humor, he concluded that all he could find was a huge, burly security guard. "Sir, will you give me a hug?" he asked.

"I sure will!" the security guard responded. Dr. Weigelt indicated that in that affectionate hug, he found comfort and encouragement. He was able to return to his room and sleep peacefully.

Ministers, hug your family today!

faith into action

Purpose, plan, and apply a hug independently for each of your family members and any other loved ones this week.

You must do the very thing
you cannot do.
—Eleanor Roosevelt

Do you know the story of the father who loved his son, but couldn't find the time to give him attention?

The son wanted to build a tree house, but the father always seemed to have an excuse that precluded him from doing so. One day, after a serious accident, the son lay dying in the hospital. The dad was frantic to relate to his son and save his life, but as the boy's condition worsened, he knew it was hopeless.

The last words the father heard from his son were, "I'm sorry, Dad, it looks like we won't get around to building that tree house after all." How painful that must have been.

From the Lord comes deliverance. May your blessing be on your people.
—Psalm 3:8

I was guilty of getting caught up in the fast-paced schedule of pastoring, often at the expense of those I loved. So, what would I do differently if I had another chance? I would act on, not talk about, how much I loved my family. Each week, I would share a quality event with my boys. I would have a date every week—no matter what—with my wife. I would honor my family by taking a day off each week. I would not burden them so much with the challenges I faced, and I would proclaim by my actions how valuable they were to me.

Does your family know without a doubt that they are more important to you than *anything*? I pray so! But if not, ask God to show you how to make things right.

faith into action

Plan for each of your family members a date, just between the two of you, with no agenda other than to spend time together. Set the dates, arrange it with each person, and keep every date.

The great use of life is to spend it for
something that will outlast it.

—Charles Mayes

disappearance

An A-10 Thunderbolt II Air Force attack jet suddenly and
mysteriously disappeared in the Colorado mountains in
spring 1997. The pilot, Captain Craig Button, was also missing.
With each passing day of searching, the mystery surrounding
the disappearance intensified. How could a multi-million dollar
Air Force attack jet just vanish?

As I kept up with the story, a parallel struck me. What
about missing ministers? You may be one.

In our country today, there are scores of fulltime and volunteer
ministers who have dropped off the radar screen. It may have

been because they failed and were forced to go elsewhere. It might have been that life turned so sour, they decided to become reclusive.

Maybe you have chosen to withdraw from those who care for you because it's too difficult to be confronted with your calling and purpose.

We can't afford to lose another brother or sister. We must do all we can to locate those who have chosen to get lost.

Unlimited resources were used to find the lost plane. Why is it we do so little to locate our colleagues and love them back into the fold?

faith into action

Cull through your personal history of friends and colleagues in ministry—who are those that are missing in action? Prayerfully make steps to search out and find the fallen.

I once was lost, but now I'm found!
—John Newton in "Amazing Grace"

When I spoke once at a Christian university, the preliminaries were long and the room was warm. As the proceedings continued, I was led to change my message to a more passionate appeal for the lost to come to the saving grace of Jesus Christ.

While waiting, my thoughts turned to a drive-thru tour of another university. There, I had seen hundreds of students on campus and was prompted by the Holy Spirit to wonder, "How many of these students know Jesus Christ as Savior?"

I was emotional as I addressed the group at this school, because it dawned on me that in this world of the church we

How, then, can they call on the one they have not believed in? And how can they believe in the one of whom they have not heard? And how can they hear without someone preaching to them? And how can they preach unless they are sent? As it is written, "How beautiful are the feet of those who bring good news!"
—Romans 10:14–15

have a tendency to look more *at what we have, rather than what we don't have*. In the world that's okay, but in the kingdom of God I don't think it is.

There was a day in the church when the salvation message was the number one priority. I wonder if it still is. Is it with you?

The passion to lead the lost into a found condition must become paramount in all of our ministries if the nation and the world are to experience genuine revival.

faith into action

Ask God to help you objectively examine your heart and discern your passion for the lost. Is it authentically there, or is it forced . . . a duty? Ask God to put faces to your passion (or lack of it)—that you may truly be motivated to act by his strength, not your own.

For information on seminars, scheduling
speaking engagements, or to contact the author:

Stan Toler
P. O. Box 892170
Oklahoma City, OK 73189-2170
www.stantoler.com